The Secret Language
of Herbs

The Secret Language
of Herbs

ALICE PECK

CICO BOOKS
LONDON NEW YORK

FOR DUANE AND TYL

Published in 2018 by CICO Books
An imprint of Ryland Peters & Small Ltd

20–21 Jockey's Fields,
London WC1R 4BW

341 E 116th St,
New York, NY 10029

www.rylandpeters.com

10 9 8 7 6 5 4 3 2 1

Text © Alice Peck 2018

Design and illustration
© CICO Books 2018

A CIP catalog record for this book is
available from the Library of Congress
and the British Library.

ISBN: 978-1-78249-559-8

Printed in China

Editor: **Dawn Bates**
Designer: **Paul Tilby**
Illustrator: **Sarah Perkins**

Commissioning editor:
Kristine Pidkameny
Senior editor: **Carmel Edmonds**
Art director: **Sally Powell**
Head of production: **Patricia Harrington**
Publishing manager: **Penny Craig**
Publisher: **Cindy Richards**

IMAGE CREDITS

All images under license from Shutterstock. **Back cover/p. 75:** Spline_x; **p. 1/p. 101:** Henrik Larsson;
p. 2/p. 119: Maya Kruchankova, Colnihko, Kotkot32; **p. 3/p. 83:** Shiro_ring, Mariola Anna S;
p. 8/p. 29: Ed Samuel; **p. 10:** Photowind, Heike Brauer; **p. 13:** Nataliia Melnychuk; **p. 14:** Madeleine
Steinbach, Daniel Prudek; **p. 17:** Anna Gratys; **p. 19:** Evgenii Urlapov, Costea Anda M, Linda
George; **p. 20:** Kuttelvaserova Stuchelova, Olga Pink; **p. 24:** Volodymyr Nikitenko, Snowbelle;
p. 27: Woo Jung Hoon; **p. 30:** Wasanajai, Marina Onokhina; **p. 33:** Artdig; **p. 35:** Alis Photo,
Madlen, Luka Hercigonja; **p. 37:** Gordana Sermek; **p. 38:** Le Do, Alp Aksoy, Iasmina Calinciuc;
p. 41: Inizia, Swapan Photography, picturepartners; **p. 42/p. 69:** Belokoni Dmitri, Quanthem,
Volosina; **p. 44:** nice_pictures; **p. 47:** Anna-Mari West, Romrodphoto; **p. 49:** Liv friis-Larsen, Kazu
Inoue; **p. 50:** Bon Appetit, Swapan Photography, Nanka, Lewal 1988; **p. 53:** Sergei Drozd, Anna
Grigorjeva; **p. 54:** Spline_x; **p. 58:** Scisetti Alfio, Hortimages; **p. 61:** Dani Vincek, Heike Rau;
p. 62: Dokmaihaeng; **p. 65:** Anastasia Davydova, Sandra Standbridge; **p. 66:** Angelakatharina, Scisetti
Alfio; **p. 71:** Werner Spiess, ChWeiss, Manfred Ruckszio; **p. 72/p. 78:** Geo-grafika, Scisetti Alfio,
Vilor, picturepartners; **p. 77:** ArjaKo's, Hildaweges Photography; **p. 81:** Pilialoha, images and videos,
Valery Vishnevsky; **p. 84:** LutsenkoLarissa, 13Smile; **p. 87:** Spline_x, Soyka, SeDmi; **p. 91:** Scisetti
Alfio, PattyOrly, Vetre; **p. 92:** Mamsizz, Marc Parsons; **p. 95:** Emberiza, Heike Rau, Hichako_t;
p. 96/p. 123: Kostrez, Jan Faukner; **p. 98:** Masha_Semenova, JurateBuiviene; **p. 103:** Rootstock,
Fablok, AMV_80; **p. 104:** Cafe Racer, Shansh23, Jeanie333, tbodin; **p. 106:** Natalila K, Oizostudio,
Thanthima Lim; **p. 109:** Chang-Pooh24, Coloa Studio, Sommai; **p. 111:** Ikonya, ChameleonsEye,
Solkanar; **p. 115:** Lutic, Beas777; **p. 116:** Oxik, Racobovt; **p. 120:** Mau47, Christian Musst;
p. 125: Marie C Fields, Brent Hofacker, Stoica ionela, 5PH, Kaiskynet.

CONTENTS

Introduction 6

Introduction

Herbs, like flowers, speak a special language all their own. It is one of healing and hope, love and joy, protection and guidance, ritual and promise. In studying this language, we discover a wisdom for body, mind, and spirit that is as deep-rooted as the beginning of the written word and as current as recent scientific research. The herbal lexicon grows from art, religion, poetry, sacred teaching, and history to connect and capture our imagination.

Many of us are familiar with the secret language of flowers, based on the Victorian practice of sending bouquets that conveyed coded vocabularies, but myriad insights give special meanings to herbs as well. These come from diverse sources and traditions—ancient Greek, Egyptian, Tibetan, Native American, and Persian texts; the writing of botanists, explorers, and naturalists; Ayurveda, Shakespeare, the Bible, folklore, modern medicine, shamanism, and many more.

Webster's Dictionary defines an herb as "a plant valued for its medicinal, savory, or aromatic qualities." The language of herbs goes beyond that, giving a significance to plants both common and exotic as they become symbols for a richer understanding. Each herb in this book offers a way of taking something from our garden, kitchen, or ambles in the woods and looking at it in a new light, imbuing it with significance. Each speaks to us in its own distinct voice—of wellness, celebration, relationships, and sacrament—and we with them as we incorporate herbs into our homes, spiritual practices, gardens, and food.

Healing & Hope

Evening Primrose

A s if "evening primrose" weren't already a lovely name, this herb's other appellations are just as poetic: night willow, king's cure-all, evening star. It deserves them all—with its clusters of yellow or pink flowers, evening primrose is an eye-catching plant, made even more special because each flower opens at dusk, and for only one night, making it a favorite in Victorian moonlight gardens. Evening primrose is one of the fastest blooming plants, taking less than a minute to transform from bud to a blossom some 2in (5cm) wide, and if you time it correctly you can watch one (or several) open right before your eyes. By morning, the flower is nothing more than a withered memory.

Evening primrose grows wild throughout the United States, sometimes as tall as 9ft (3m). Native Americans and early colonists ate the seeds, roots, and leaves, drank the tea, and made poultices from the leaves. Modern herbalists use the oil to treat heart disease, arthritis, and the mood swings and other cyclical symptoms related to premenstrual syndrome (PMS).

The key to the evening primrose's current popularity is the concentration of the oil found in the seeds—the essential fatty acid gamma-linolenic acid (GLA), an omega-6, which is essential for health, but not produced by the human body. Current research is seeing promise in evening primrose oil for heart disease, skin conditions, and certain types of cancers.

If you love evening primrose... you're an optimistic person who takes delight in a certain amount of mystery and seems to find poetry everywhere.

Arnica

Arnica plants resemble small bright yellow sunflowers with velvety leaves. This perennial herb grows wild in the alpine meadows and woods of central Europe, the Pyrenees, Russia, and North America, often the only bright spot of color in a rocky landscape.

A favorite herb in homeopathy—a micro-dosing technique based on the belief that like cures like—arnica creams and salves are used as an analgesic to treat muscle aches, sprains, bruises, and arthritis. This is why it's sometimes known as "tumbler's cure all." Tubes of arnica cream can often be found in first-aid kits and gym bags. In his 1880 *Comprehensive Medical Dictionary*, Dr. J. Thomas terms it *panace'a lapso'rum* or the panacea of the fallen. Although I've found references to it as "leopard's bane" going as far back as the 18th century, no source seems to answer why.

It is called "mountain tobacco" as the leaves can be dried and smoked as a tobacco substitute the French call *tabac des Vosges*, but I wouldn't recommend it. Another name translates as sneezewort, because freshly cut crushed flowers will tickle the nose and cause sneezing. It's said that German philosopher Johann Wolfgang von Goethe drank arnica tea to ease his chest pains, but it must have been in quite small doses because taking arnica internally can be quite toxic.

Some attribute great powers to arnica, advising that if you want to change the weather, burn arnica leaves and recite: "Set arnica alight, thunderstorm take flight."

If you love arnica... you're energetic and not afraid to take risks and push yourself to your limits. Your reliability and zeal inspire even the most apathetic person.

"As sweet as Balm, as soft as air, as gentle."

WILLIAM SHAKESPEARE, FROM *ANTONY AND CLEOPATRA*

Lemon Balm

Lemon balm is often referred to as melissa—a name derived from the Greek for honey bee—as well as bee balm and bee pepper, so it's no surprise it's a favorite of our apiarian friends. As Pliny the Elder wrote, "When they are strayed away, they do find their way home by it."

Native to the Mediterranean, this bushy perennial, with unremarkable white flowers yet a lovely and certainly remarkable fragrance, was dedicated to the goddess Diana by the ancient Greeks and used medicinally for its calming properties. It's also a staple of Chinese medicine and a main ingredient along with lemon peel, nutmeg, and angelica root, in Carmelite water, a French distilled alcohol digestive originally prepared by 14th-century Carmelite nuns of the Abbey of St Just, which is still available today.

"Balm is sovereign for the brain, strengthening the memory and powerfully chasing away melancholy," wrote John Evelyn (1620–1706). A 2004 study of lemon balm carried out at Northumbria University in Newcastle, England verified this. The students who consumed lemon balm before taking tests were less anxious and scored considerably better than those given a placebo. Drinking the tea can lift depression, soothe melancholy, reduce stress, and ease sleep.

According to 19th-century herbalist Mrs M. Grieve, John Hussey, of Sydenham, England who lived to be 116, breakfasted for the last half of his life on lemon balm tea and honey and gave it credit for his longevity.

It's said that if you carry lemon balm leaves in your pocket you'll find your love, and carrying the buds will mend a broken heart.

If you love lemon balm...you're compassionate, empathetic, and love to laugh. You attract sweetness and bring out the best in people.

Wintergreen

Wintergreen's tiny waxy white flower is followed by a bright red berry, hence its names such as spice berry, checker berry, teaberry, box berry, partridge berry, and deer berry. It's a familiar minty flavoring used in candies, chewing gum, toothpaste, mouthwash, and even root beer. In 1857, American perfumer G.W. Septimus Piesse wrote of wintergreen: "A perfuming otto [essential oil] can be procured by distilling the leaves of this plant: it is principally consumed in the perfuming of soaps. Upon the strength of the name of this odorous plant a very nice handkerchief perfume is made."

Indigenous to North America, from Georgia to Newfoundland, and found throughout Europe, including the British Isles and Scandinavia, this creeping evergreen loves woodlands and mountains. Its seeds are among the smallest in the plant kingdom: 250,000 seeds can be contained in a single gram.

Native Americans brewed a tea from the leaves to reduce bodily aches and pains, fever, and sore throat. The oil is included in liniments and salves for arthritis and sore joints. There is a science behind this as wintergreen contains salicylic acid, a proven non-steroidal anti-inflammatory drug (NSAID) like aspirin.

Wintergreen is traditionally put in children's pillowcases for protection and good luck. The fresh sprigs are said to be healing and a summons to good spirits. Wintergreen is grown, dried, and burned like an incense to attract well-being.

If you love wintergreen... you're optimistic and resilient. You are careful to tend to the needs of other people and yourself. You savor the richness of life and help others experience it as well.

Echinacea

VIGOR | SANCTUARY | FORTITUDE

Echinacea is derived from the Greek word *echinos*, describing a hedgehog or sea urchin, reflecting the texture of the herb's seed cone at the center of its regal purple flowers. Beloved of butterflies and bees and even small birds, echinacea is also called purple coneflower, Sampson root, whip plant, and elk root.

Folklore says echinacea offers fortitude during trying times and if kept in a home will ensure money in the bank. It is one of the most popular herbal remedies in the United States and Europe, relied upon for strengthening the immune system to fight flus, infections, and colds—or at least lessen their duration.

Native to the woodlands and prairies of North America, it's said that when Native Americans of the Great Plains observed sick or wounded deer or elk foraging for the plants and recovering after eating them, they began to try it for themselves. Hence "elk root" was soon added to their medicine kit to treat insect and snakebites as well as rabies.

Joseph Meyer, a 19th-century purveyor of patent medicines, claimed to have learned about the powers of echinacea from the Native Americans. He sold an echinacea tincture as a panacea for all ailments, from which we get the term "snake oil salesman," for someone who is selling a quack medicine.

If you love echinacea... you are practical with a quirky side. Although not always the most patient person, your determination fosters your accomplishments and when you put your mind to a task you always excel.

Comfrey

Comfrey's bell-shaped flowers are blue, purple, or white, although its hairy leaves are perhaps not the prettiest in the garden. In Latin, it is called *con firmo* or make firm because it was believed comfrey poultices would speed the healing of broken bones. Its Greek designation *Symphytum* combines "grow together" and "plant" and like many of comfrey's other names—knit-bone, healing herb, bone-heal, bruise-wort, knit back, and miracle herb—reveals the herb's reputation.

Although prescribed as such by a 16th-century herbalist, it might not be the best treatment for a broken bone, although mashed and wrapped around an injury it dried like a cast until replaced by plaster. It's not all lore—comfrey contains allantoin, which promotes skin regrowth and contains anti-inflammatory properties, so a liniment might be just the thing for a scrape or bruise. Modern herbalists recommend a salve made from comfrey roots for aches and pains (but for external use only).

It's said that if you carry a bit of comfrey with you when you travel it will ensure a safe journey, so consider slipping some in your backpack or suitcase the next time you venture off.

It's the flower associated with the feast day of the Armenian St John the Silent (CE 424–558), who shunned fame and lived in the wilderness for over 70 years, not speaking, but rather listening to God.

If you love comfrey... you're a bit cautious yet diplomatic, the "strong, silent type" in the best sense. You respect privacy and can be relied upon to keep a secret.

Chamomile

This fragrant herb has flowers like miniature daisies. It smells and tastes a bit like apple, so it makes sense that the Ancient Greeks named this low-growing plant "earth apple" and the Spanish call it *manzanilla* or "little apple." The Germans describe chamomile as *alles tutraut*, which means "capable of anything" and it seems there's very little this versatile herb can't do.

Many of us first encountered chamomile tea in Beatrix Potter's *The Tale of Peter Rabbit*. When Peter returned home after his misadventures in Mr McGregor's cabbage patch, his mother gave him a few sips to calm him before putting him to bed. Modern science supports her practice. A compound found in chamomile—*apigenin*—acts as a sedative and eases anxiety. Chamomile is a tonic and cure-all used to aid digestion, and to treat colds, arthritis, and insomnia.

As long as it doesn't overtake the flowerbed, gardeners love chamomile because it keeps away pests, and if grown near sickly plants rejuvenates them. It's often sown into lawns or entrances of gardens so that visitors will *have* to step on it. This is because a little trampling helps chamomile thrive, by releasing its apple-like fragrance and encouraging it to grow. Perhaps because it does well with being stepped on, one of the meanings of this "herb of humility" is "energy in adversity."

If you love chamomile... you're resilient and multidimensional, optimistic and patient, peaceful and modest. You're grounded, able to weather the complexities of life, to find the calm within the storm, the glimmer of sunlight on the darkest day.

"...chamomile, the more it is trodden,
the faster it grows; yet youth, the more
it is wasted, the sooner it wears."

WILLIAM SHAKESPEARE, FROM *KING HENRY IV, PART 1*

Valerian

It goes by many names: capon's tail, all-heal, bloody butcher, cat's valerian, fragrant valerian, garden heliotrope, St George's herb, vandal root, and set-wale because it can be found growing by ruined wales or walls. The genus name *valere* comes from the Latin "to be well or strong or powerful." Ancient Greeks believed it could reverse bad and make it good.

This perennial plant, with long hollow stems ending in clusters of sweet-scented flowers ranging in color from the very palest to bright pink, is sometimes called "herbal valium." It's a traditional remedy for nervous tension and insomnia, the root is used medicinally, and the tea makes a strong sedative that promotes calm and sleep, working as a depressant on the central nervous system but without the side-effects of narcotics.

Another common name for valerian is phu—as in "Phew! That's stinky!" Indeed, although its pretty flowers bloom all summer, it is not a sweet-smelling herb and historically it has been used to bait rodent traps. It has been theorized that the Pied Piper of Hamelin's ability to charm and lure rats had more to do with pockets full of valerian than his musical gifts.

Perhaps it's not just rodents it attracts. It's thought to be an aphrodisiac and is used as an ingredient in "love sachets." In medieval times, it was said that if a woman wore the scent of valerian, men would follow her "like children."

If you love valerian... you are even-keeled, content, self-accepting, and free from guilt. Your lack of neuroses allows you to do your best in all situations.

Ginseng

With its small white flowers, and shiny red berries, ginseng is so treasured for its healing capabilities that wars have been fought over it. Of the genus *Panax*—for panacea or all-healing—it's valued for its adaptogenic quality and the belief that ginseng helps the body adjust to cold, stress, and fatigue. It's used throughout the world to treat everything from colic to dementia.

The root has long been sought and used in Chinese medicine. It's said that the more the ginseng root looks like a human body, the greater its healing capabilities. In fact, the Chinese word *Jin-chen* is composed of characters for "likeness of man," describing the link between spirit and human, as well as how the roots take on the form of legs and arms. One Chinese legend tells of how ginseng is the result of the ongoing heavenly battle between water and fire—when lightning strikes a pure stream, ginseng is formed, embodying the elemental forces of the universe.

Whereas Asian ginseng is considered "hot" and mildly stimulating, the American variety is "cool" and more of a tonic. The Native Americans knew its healing power as did the colonial Americans, including Benjamin Franklin.

It's not just a physical healing. An element of shamanic rituals throughout Asia and among Native Americans, ginseng has been imbued with magical properties as well. It's said that carrying a piece of ginseng as a charm will bring beauty and love, ward off evil, and grant wishes.

If you love ginseng... you're a person of clear judgment and vision. You're able to weigh all sides of a situation to determine the best outcome.

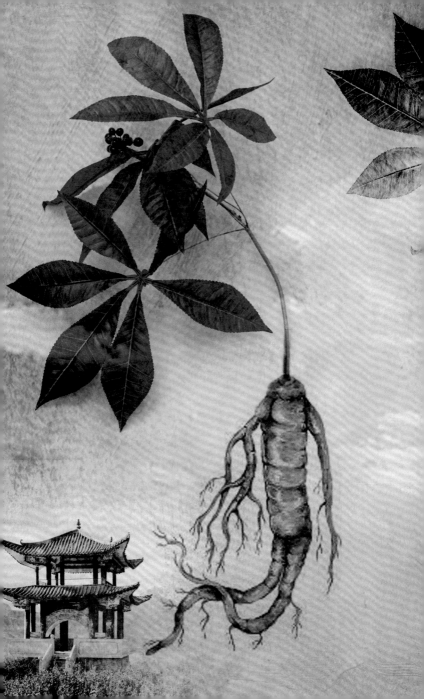

Feverfew

Feverfew's pretty daisy-like flowers smell a bit like camphor—a strong odor that repels insects, but unfortunately this includes honeybees. It is a tall plant—growing up to 3ft (1m)—with attractive dark green leaves. It is also known as flirt-wort, bachelor's button, feather-few, midsummer daisy, and wild chamomile, as well as feather-foil, which became featherfew and then feverfew in the Middle Ages.

Although once used as a fever reducer (as reflected in its name) and to prevent malaria, feverfew was found ineffectual, so it is no longer employed for those purposes.

During the first century, the Greek physician Dioscorides noted its anti-inflammatory and febrifuge (fever-reducing) properties. Sacred to the goddess Athena, a Greek myth tells of Zeus concocting a brew containing feverfew to charm the remarkably handsome Trojan hero Ganymede to lure him to Olympus where he could be his cupbearer for eternity.

Traditionally a "women's herb," it was used as a sedative to treat malaise and vertigo, and prevent migraine headaches. Clinical trials by the City of London Migraine Clinic and University Hospital in Nottingham, UK, demonstrated this to be true, finding that it did not cure migraines, but it prevented and reduced their severity by about 24 percent. Perhaps this is because feverfew inhibits the release of histamines and controls serotonin levels, which are thought to trigger migraines. Use caution, as feverfew is related to ragweed and if you're allergic to that pollen you might be allergic to feverfew as well and end up worsening the problems you're trying to solve.

If you love feverfew... you look for a solution in all situations. You're not one to give up quickly and are relied on for your open mind.

Purslane

A denizen of vacant lots and pavement cracks and often found in rubbish heaps, many see purslane as a weed, best pulled up and fed to swine. Hence some of its names: pigweed and little hogweed. Yet others have recognized its nobility and power—it was carried by soldiers for protection in battle—calling it Blood of Ares after the ancient Greek god of war.

Purslane was crushed into a variety of healing poultices in Europe, Iran, and India. Native Americans used it for burns, earaches, and headaches. Many cultures recommend it as a treatment for wasp stings and lizard bites. The tender leaves are delicious—lemony and peppery—and contain more vitamin E than spinach, more betacarotene than carrots, and are packed with many other nutrients, especially omega-3 antioxidants.

Henry David Thoreau wrote in *Walden*: "I have made a satisfactory dinner, satisfactory on several accounts, simply off a dish of purslane *(Portulaca oleracea)* which I gathered in my cornfield, boiled and salted. I give the Latin on account of the savoriness of the trivial name."

Purslane is a herb said to spread luck, joy, and love, and to ward off evil if sprinkled throughout the home, perhaps because of its inherent powers or abilities to nourish and sustain—either way it's definitely one to befriend.

If you love purslane... your versatility is an asset. You don't crave attention, but you don't shun it either. You're the kind of person everyone can connect with in one way or the other.

Devil's Claw

A member of the sesame family, devil's claw has purple and pink trumpet-shaped flowers. Because of its strange spikey fruit, it is called *Harpagophytum procumbens*—the "creeping grappling iron plant."

An "angel of a pain reliever" is how health writer Michael Castleman describes devil's claw in *The New Healing Herbs*. An angiosperm, it's a traditional medicine of the San people of the Kalahari. Devil's claw roots are now used worldwide as a safe and effective supplement to reduce pain, particularly in the lower back and as an anti-inflammatory for joint pain, arthritis, and rheumatism.

This fruit's form follows function and seems to have developed to facilitate germination in the loose sand of the savannah, where there is the constant threat of the seeds being carried away by the wind. It's said that these seed pods can be used as charms to protect one from evil—again, the claw-like form suggesting the purpose.

Of all devil's claw's many names, the one I like best is wood spider—which describes the way its silvery leaves trail horizontally and low to the ground. This perennial flourishes in the dry rocky soil and grasslands of Angola, Namibia, the Kalahari region, South Africa, Zimbabwe, and Botswana, where it is the nation's floral emblem.

If you love devil's claw... you are steadfast and determined. You tend to get what you want if you put your mind to it, which you always do. You are fiercely protective of those near and dear to you.

St John's-wort

Native to Europe and Britain, the many names for St John's-wort are evocative and varied: amber, goat-weed, Klamath weed, devil's flight, Tipton weed, hard-hay, rosin rose, grace of God, and witches' herb. Its flowers are a cheery yellow-gold, the prominent stamens giving them an almost fuzzy appearance.

Its Greek name, *hypericum*, comes from the words *hyper* (above) and *eikon* (picture) describing the custom of hanging St John's-wort on religious icons to celebrate the Feast of St John the Baptist. It was also burned in bonfires on this holiday, which coincides with the summer solstice.

St John's-wort has been attributed with magical properties since at least the Middle Ages when it was used to purify homes, drive away malevolent witches and ghosts, and protect crops. It was hung over doors and windows and given to the sick to wear in amulets as a defense against the evil eye.

The 17th-century botanist Nicholas Culpeper was on to something when he described St John's-wort as a treatment for mental disorders: "The decoction of the leaves and seeds drank somewhat warm before the fits of agues...alters the fits, and, by often using, doth take them quite away." Traditionally used to treat emotional and nervous problems, modern herbalists recommend St John's-wort and researchers are ascertaining how it works as a curative for mild to moderate depression.

If you love St John's-wort... you're a deep thinker and perhaps a bit introverted. Some say you lead a charmed life, but you know it's because you're able to see the magic in even the simplest of things.

Marshmallow

A favorite of hummingbirds, with its large blossoms in varieties of white, pink, and pale violet, marshmallow is a cheery flowering herb reminiscent of the hollyhock and is indigenous to Europe, Western Asia, and North Africa. It flourishes in damp soil, boggy meadows, and tidal rivers—the marshes from which its name comes.

Marshmallow's genus, *Althaea*, comes from the Greek, meaning "to cure." It is mentioned in the Book of Job and Pliny wrote, "Whosoever shall take a spoonful of the Mallows, shall that day be free of all diseases that may come to him." It was also prescribed by Ancient India's Ayurvedic physicians. It is still an effective treatment for coughs and a gargle for sore throats because of its high mucilage content, which soothes the mucous membranes.

In the mid-1800s a clever French person peeled a marshmallow root, boiled it in sugar, and *voila!* the marshmallow was invented. Nowadays, it's a mass-manufactured air-puffed concoction of sugar, water, gelatin, and cornstarch, containing none of the plant from which it gets its name. If you're crafty, you can buy marshmallow powder and make them yourself—there are hundreds of recipes on the Internet.

Dried marshmallow roots, called *hochets de guimauve*, are still sold in France. They're used to soothe babies who are teething. The fibrous root softens as the child gums it, releasing the sweet and soothing pith.

On the Isle of Man, it was believed that marshmallow could undo a fairy's spell.

If you love marshmallow... you are kind and gentle, patient, and sweet. You want the best for everyone and endeavor to achieve this.

"Anyse maketh the breth sweter and swageth payne."

WILLIAM TURNER, FROM *A NEW HERBALL* (1551)

Anise

A delicate annual, with feathery leaves and lacy white flowers, the fragrant seeds its blossoms produce are what make anise so special. Ancient Roman feasts concluded with an aniseed cake as an aid to digestion and because it was thought to be an aphrodisiac. Whether or not anise seeds can spark romance, they are a delightful component in cookies: German *Pfeffernüsse* and *Springerle*, Australian humbugs, Italian *pizzelle*, and Peruvian *picarones*. Anise is used in all sorts of candies and is what makes black jelly beans taste like... well... black jelly beans. It perfumes liquors like Pernod, arak, ouzo, Sambuca, and even absinthe and some root beers.

Not merely delicious, this aromatic herb is rich in phenylpropanoids, which have anti-inflammatory capabilities. It is used to settle an upset stomach and as an after-dinner digestive. A few teaspoons of cool anise tea can calm a colicky baby. Like so many herbs, anise was first cultivated in the Middle East and found its way across the Mediterranean because of its medicinal usefulness.

A sachet of anise seeds tucked into a pillow is said to ward off bad dreams. Some think it averts the evil eye. According to Scott Cunningham's *Encyclopedia of Magical Herbs*, anise seed "is used to call forth spirits to aid in magical operations, and a sprig hung on the bedpost will restore lost youth." There's certainly no harm in trying, especially because the process will smell so sweet.

If you love anise... you balance your confidence with humility. You're hopeful and cheerful—seeing the sweet things in life—and are never afraid to face a challenge. You know when to pause and take care of yourself. And of course, you love licorice!

Fenugreek

With tiny white flowers and long pointy seedpods that reflect one of its names—cow's horn—fenugreek is also known as bird's-foot violet and Greek hay (or the Latin *foenumg raecum*) because it was used to refresh musty fodder. Rich in iron, it is a member of the pea family and its leaves (called *methi*) are a food staple in Indian and Pakistani cuisines. The seeds are a key ingredient in curry throughout southwest Asia and are also used in North African, Persian, and Eastern Mediterranean cooking.

Native to the Middle East, it is mentioned in the *Ebers Papyrus*—one of the oldest Egyptian medical compilations from about 1550 BCE—as a treatment for burns. Fenugreek may also have been used for embalming mummies. Multiple sources refer to fenugreek seeds excavated from Tell Halal in Iraq and carbon-dated to 4000 BCE. Hippocrates valued it for its soothing capabilities and ninth-century Benedictine monks popularized fenugreek in Europe. Considered a folk cure for pretty much any purpose—including increasing a breastfeeding mother's milk—modern studies have shown that the herb can help control cholesterol and blood sugar levels in diabetes.

It is said that growing a small pot of fenugreek in your home, carrying a few seeds in your pocket, or adding a few seeds to the rinse water when you are cleaning your house will attract money. Although this can't be proven, even the simplest results—a pretty plant and a fragrant home—are rewards unto themselves.

If you love fenugreek... you're reliable and persistent, the kind of person who doesn't waver. You're fond of travel but equally happy when settled with your home comforts.

Love & Joy

Basil

A favorite in many kitchens, basil can be sweet or holy. It's most commonly an annual with its bright green leaves and spikes of tiny white blossoms. A member of the mint family, it originated in Africa, was domesticated in India, and spread around the globe from there. Its 150 varieties are known by many names including St Joseph's-wort, king of herbs, the royal herb, kiss-me-Nicholas, and *tulsi*.

The ancient Greeks thought basil was poisonous, but the Romans deemed that the fragrance encouraged passion. If a Roman maiden grew basil on her balcony, it was an invitation to her lover to visit.

Sacred to the Tulasi, Hindu goddess of fidelity, purity, and devotion, basil is often planted around temples and used in burials. Likewise, the Haitians associate basil with Erzulie, the Voodoo spirit of love, beauty, and flowers, and it served as a symbol of betrothal in old Rumania.

Basil is a magical predictor of love. Pluck two fresh basil leaves and place them on a hot ember, perhaps in your fireplace. If the basil burns smoothly and turns to ash, your relationship will be a happy one; if it jumps and crackles, expect squabbles or worse.

The fragrance of basil is said to create empathy. It is believed to bring money to those who carry it in their pockets and good luck if given as a housewarming gift.

Basil has great curative powers, from asthma to canker sores to infections, and there's science to support this as the oil contains antimicrobial qualities.

If you love basil... you are brave, altruistic, always wishing the best for others. You're the kind of person who loves to love.

Lavender

ATTENTIVENESS | CONSCIENTIOUSNESS | CONSTANCY

Lavender is such a romantic herb. It's associated with purity, sweetness, virtue, and undying love, so it's no wonder that it is thought to be an aphrodisiac. Clothing scented with lavender is said to bring romance to the wearer and rubbing it on stationery before writing a love letter is said to give power to an amorous connection.

From the Latin meaning "to be washed", the oil and flowers have been used to scent bath- and wash-water since ancient times. As a tea, lavender is wonderful for relaxing, especially paired with chamomile. It's a favorite for aromatherapy as well, and when inhaled, the volatile compounds seem to act via the limbic system, particularly the amygdala and hippocampus, to calm the mind and abate stress. (But don't overdo it with lavender or you may cloud your memory.)

Given as a gift, lavender promises new beginnings and opportunities. A sprig may bring good luck, confuse witches, and allow the bearer to see ghosts. Lavender scattered in corners brings peace to a home. Lore tells of how when the Virgin Mary laundered the swaddling clothes of the infant Jesus and hung them to dry on a lavender bush, lavender took on the scent of Heaven.

It's especially attractive when grown in large patches or hedges so that both the color of the blossoms and the perfume are intensified. The flowers are most potent if picked on sunny midsummer mornings. Tuck a sprig of lavender into your pillow and fall asleep thinking of a wish. If you dream about it, your wish will come true. Perhaps this (along with the heady aroma) is why lavender pillows are so popular and pleasing.

If you love lavender... you are a steady friend, persevering, and joyful at any task. You are content, happy, and devoted to all that you love.

"Lavender's green, dilly, dilly,
Lavender's blue.
You must love me, dilly, dilly,
'cause I love you."

ENGLISH FOLK SONG
(17TH CENTURY)

Myrtle

Myrtle has a sweet, spicy fragrance, star-shaped flowers, and dark berries. The essential oil, for external use, is an antiseptic. A symbol of peace and joy in the Old Testament, it is one of the four sacred plants for the Feast of the Tabernacles. In English folklore, dreaming of seeing a blooming myrtle foretells many lovers, a large family, wealth, and long life.

The fifth-century Greek traveler Herodotus, wrote of myrtle: "The hero wore it as a mark of victory; the bridegroom, on his bridal day; and friends presented each other with myrtle garlands, in the conviviality of the banquet. Venus is said to have been adorned with it, when Paris decided in her favor the prize of beauty…"

Brides still wear wreaths of myrtle leaves to symbolize love, purity, and fertility. Since Queen Victoria, the bouquets of British royal brides have included myrtle grown from a bush in the gardens of Windsor Castle and the source of the myrtle Queen Victoria carried on her wedding day.

There's a lovely saying from the county of Somerset in England: "The flowering myrtle is the luckiest plant to have in your window; Water it every morning and be proud of it." It's said that blackbirds use myrtle twigs in their nests to protect the chicks from evil. A French superstition suggests that a myrtle will only take root if planted on Good Friday. And legends across Europe deem myrtle a harbinger of good luck.

If you love myrtle… you're devoted to your relationships, faithful, and loyal. You're lucky in life and in love and do your best to share your gifts with others.

Cardamom

With elegant pale blue flowers, cardamom, also called "grains of paradise," is a natural Ayurveda tranquilizer. It is said to bring clarity and joy to the heart and mind and known to aid digestion. Part of the ginger family, there are many varieties of cardamom, including white, green, black, and red, as well as Java, Siamese, Bengal, and Kravan.

Native to India, Nepal, and Sri Lanka, cardamom was believed to have been brought to Europe by Alexander the Great. Before World War I it was introduced by German coffee planters to Guatemala, which is now the largest producer. It's the world's most expensive spice after saffron and vanilla because it is so difficult to grow.

Considered a powerful aphrodisiac, it is recommended that those looking for love chew cardamom seeds, burn them like incense, or add them to sachets and put them in linen cabinets or the clothes dryer. Perhaps it's the freshened breath or the heady fragrance that contributes to the romance, but it is pleasant regardless.

Known in Hindi as *ilaichi*, it is an aromatic primary ingredient in curry and masala in the East, and cookies and pastries in the West. Adding cardamom pods or a pinch of powder to coffee as you are roasting or brewing it is a symbol of hospitality and may prevent the jitters often brought on by caffeine. To aid digestion, boil cardamom in warm milk, add a little honey, and drink before bedtime. Cardamom is especially delightful in chai.

If you love cardamom... you are warmhearted and devoted. You have an active mind and tend toward optimism. You always welcome a good story or new idea.

Dandelion

Dandelion comes from the French *dent-de-lion* perhaps because the jagged leaves recall a lion's teeth. It's called puff-ball and blowball, for its cottony tops when it goes to seed. In 1878, Ralph Waldo Emerson wrote, "What is a weed? A plant whose virtues have yet to be discovered." This is certainly the case with the dandelion.

This herb has magical powers, and in the Victorian language of flowers is called the "rustic oracle." You can make a wish by blowing the seed fluff and even follow them to your good fortune. If you do so while sending thoughts to a sweetheart, it will draw them to you. Some say it's bad luck to dream about dandelions, but if an aspiring bride puts them under her pillow she'll dream of her future husband.

Dandelion is referred to in the texts of Arab physicians in the 11th century and the physicians of Myddfai in Wales in the 13th century, and was a food staple for many indigenous Americans. The young leaves are delicious in salads and the dried roots are a satisfying coffee substitute. Dandelion is nourishing, an excellent digestive aid, and a detoxifying herb.

Dandelions may also predict the weather—hence another nickname: weather clock. When the down fluffs the weather will be good, but rain is on the way if dandelions look droopy and wilted. The yellow flowers close right before a rainstorm or a heavy dew.

If you love dandelion... you're insightful and practical, with just enough dreaminess to find delight in the whimsical.

Catnip

It's said that if you clutch a catnip leaf in your hand until it's warm, the next person whose hand you hold will be your friend forever, as long as you don't lose the leaf.

"If you set it, the cats will eat it, and if you sow it, the cats don't know it." This saying seems to be true—cats will come to catnip plants that have been moved (and so probably bruised to release the scent), but not to those sown from seed and left untouched. Not just house cats, but most felines—lions, tigers, leopards, jaguars, bobcats, and lynx—fall under catnip's spell and roll in the leaves in delight, getting a little zany. It's said that giving catnip to a cat will create a psychic bond between you and the pet. Bees and butterflies are drawn to it as well, but rats and mice hate it, so it's a great thing to plant in your garden. Wild catnip has spikes of small white flowers and the garden version has blue flowers that bloom all summer long.

Catnip brings one kind of joy to felines and yet another to humans: calm and peace of mind. Studies by New York University's Langone Medical Center name nepetalactone as the active ingredient in catnip that produces its stress-relieving effect on those who sip catnip tea. Catnip also has a slight hallucinogenic effect when smoked. Stuffing pillows with dried catnip leaves is a folk treatment for insomnia and catnip tea is used to calm fevers. Herbalists prescribe it for bronchitis.

If you love catnip... you're lively and not afraid to take risks. You have a wonderful imagination and people are drawn to you and tend to fall under your spell.

Rosemary

Rosemary's fragrance is a heady combination of pine and eucalyptus. It speaks to us of love and death, but most of all the power of memory.

Legend has it that on the flight from Egypt the Virgin Mary hung her cloak over a rosemary bush and the flowers turned from white to the blue of her garment, hence the name: Rose of Mary. The Latin term is *rosmarinus*, literally "dew of the sea"—this makes sense given it is fond of sandy Mediterranean shores.

In the classic story, Prince Charming brushed Sleeping Beauty's cheek with rosemary to awaken his true love. A romance charm in Europe and England during the Middle Ages, sprigs of rosemary are still tucked into bridal bouquets today to sustain a new couple's devotion.

Rosemary is often associated with remembrance. It's a connection that spans continents and cultures and is supported by science. Rosemary contains antioxidants and has the capacity to diminish the breakdown of acetylcholine—a compound that affects parts of the brain responsible for memory and logic.

Rosemary balances joy with sorrow and has used in funerary practices since ancient times. A vestige endures—war dead are commemorated on Armistice Day by rosemary twigs pinned to lapels. Rosemary is often carried at funerals and planted on graves, perhaps because in many climates it blooms in winter—the flowers evoke the spring.

If you love rosemary... you are devoted and dedicated, thoughtful and loyal, sometimes to a fault. You see the good in all things—beginnings and endings.

"As for rosmarine,
I lette it runne all over
my garden walls, not
onlie because my bees
love it, but because it
is the herb sacred to
remembrance, and,
therefore to friendship."

SIR THOMAS MOORE (1478–1535)

"Smell of it oft, and it
shall keep thee youngly."

BANKE'S HERBAL (1525)

Chervil

This hardy herb, with fernlike leaves that turn a lovely shade of magenta in the fall, has an aromatic flavor reminiscent of tarragon. Enhancing and balancing the flavor of herbs it's combined with, chervil is a component of the French mixture *fine herbes* or *bouquet garni* with chives, tarragon, and parsley.

The 1884 *Dictionary of English Names of Plants* includes a listing for chervil as "shepherd's clock" because the shade-loving flowers open at five in the morning and close at eight in the evening, serving as botanical timekeepers.

Gerard's *Herball*, or *Generall Historie of Plantes*, published in 1597, professed that chervil "rejoiceth and comforteth the heart and increases their strength." The word chervil is derived from the Greek *chaerophyllon*, meaning "the herb of rejoicing" or "cheer leaf." And since ancient times chervil has been used to enhance digestion and flavor, and perhaps happiness as well.

In Europe, it is made into a nutritional spring tonic with dandelion and watercress, and drinking this or chervil tea is believed to restore memory and youth, cheer the spirit, ease depression, and increase vigor and well-being. In Germany, chervil soup is served on Maundy Thursday (three days before Easter) as a symbol of renewal. It's said that a basket of the seeds was found in King Tutankhamun's tomb, although this may be apocryphal, but perhaps the ancient Egyptians associated chervil with rebirth as well.

If you love chervil... you're direct, rarely fussy or prone to exaggerate. You take life as it comes, and are a delightful, easygoing, and unpretentious companion, who finds the hope and silver lining in every situation.

Lovage

Poignantly called "loveache" in Middle English, lovage is also known as love herb, wild celery, and sea parsley, and it is indeed a relative of parsley, which it resembles. Its clusters of tiny yellow or very pale green flowers blossom in the spring.

With a name like that, it's no surprise that lovage was thought to be an aphrodisiac. Putting a few spoonfuls of the herb in your bathwater is said to make you more desirable and attractive, and is a recommended practice before meeting someone new.

According to Raven Kaldera, an expert in Northern Tradition shamanism, "Lovage is much liked by Lofn, the handmaiden of Frigga, who aids warring lovers in reconciliation. It can be used in a soup or tea to help arguing, angry partners mediate and process their problems. To call on Lofn while making an offering of lovage can be a last-ditch effort before a divorce."

Celtic superstition counsels that the roots of the herb dug up on the night after Good Friday repel witches and Satan. In 1735 the Irish herbalist, John K'eogh, gave lovage credit for removing "spots, freckles, and redness from the face."

Lovage is having a resurgence of popularity as a salad herb—its taste is like celery but more intense. Interestingly, in Europe, lovage is known as the "Maggi plant" because it tastes like (although it's not an ingredient of) the popular brand of seasoning.

If you love lovage... you seek to resolve problems both large and small. You are a true romantic with a deep abiding affection for people, the arts, and all things of beauty.

"One leaf for fame,
And one for wealth
One for a faithful lover,
And one to bring glorious health..."

FOLK RHYME

Clover

According to superstition, the number of leaves on a clover is a predictor of its powers. A five-leaf clover will attract money or bad luck, depending on what you believe. Finding a three-leaf clover is a charm against witches and a symbol of the Christian Trinity, and a two-leaf clover means you will soon meet your beloved. And then there's the often sought-after four-leaf clover—said to bring good luck, ward off all sorts of sorcery and evil, enable the possessor to see fairies, and heal the sick. It's believed that four-leaf clovers spring up where the fairies step.

Clover lore doesn't end with counting leaves. If a couple eats a nibble of the same clover, that love will last forever. And if you keep clover in your shoe, it will increase your odds of falling in love with someone with lots of money. Clover wrapped in a swatch of blue silk and carried near your heart will help to mend it if it's been broken, and if you put it under your pillow you'll dream of a new love.

Clover blossoms make some of the sweetest honey and most verdant lawns, and may be the source of the phrase "living in clover." Red clover, with its distinctive pom-pom-shaped clusters of dark pink or pale violet flower heads, is especially sought out for healing. It's long been believed to be a tonic and blood purifier that flushes out toxins and strengthens the liver. This may be because red clover is a rich source of isoflavones.

If you love clover... life is good. You're easygoing, happy, and find an optimistic path through life's troubles.

Meadowsweet

SWEETNESS | HARMONY | IDLENESS

Meadowsweet's remarkably fragrant and beautiful ivory-colored blossoms are the source of its restorative qualities. Flourishing in meadows, marshes, and the moist banks of streams and ponds through most of North America, this relative of roses, almonds, and apples is sometimes called bridewort because it was strewn at weddings and crushed underfoot to release its scent. As Gerard wrote in his *Herball* (1597), "The leaves and floures of meadowsweet farre excelle all other strowing herbs for to decke up houses, to strawe in chambers, halls and banqueting houses in the summertime, for the smell thereof makes the heart merrie and joyful and delighteth the senses."

Some call it meadow queen, or lady of the meadow. Its scent is indeed sweet, a mixture of almond and vanilla, and it makes for a wonderful potpourri. Meadowsweet is beloved by bees and sweetens their honey. Sacred to the Druids, it was used to flavor mead—a fruit and honey beverage—in the Middle Ages.

In Italian, there is a phrase "*la dolce far niente*," which means the sweetness of doing nothing, and it is one I think suits meadowsweet. Although there are some herbalists who suggest it as a traditional treatment for soothing colds and nausea, and it does contain salicylic acid like aspirin, meadowsweet doesn't have much therapeutic or beneficial value compared to some of the other panacea and complex herbs.

If you love meadowsweet... you delight in peace and beauty. You're easily content—watching a quiet snowfall or sitting in the sun on a summer's day. You do your best to share that beauty with the world.

Borage

Borage, a relative of comfrey and the forget-me-not, is native to Syria and is pretty, tasty, and medicinal. It is known as a "herb of gladness," cool tankard, star flower (because of its large star-shaped blossoms), bee bread and bee fodder (because bees can't get enough of it), and ox's tongue (perhaps because of the fuzzy texture of its gray leaves). Especially nice to have in the garden, it safeguards tomato plants from pests and helps strawberries to thrive.

The English herbalist John Parkinson (1567–1650) recommended borage to "expel pensiveness and melancholie." It is often said that if you eat borage in salads you will have a happier life. With its light cucumber flavor, you'll certainly have a happy meal.

Perhaps you have heard the old saying, "I, borage, always bring courage," which is why keeping a few of these pink, blue, or purple star-shaped borage blossoms with you is said to make you brave. The flowers were embroidered on the scarves of medieval knights. Borage was mixed in wine and drunk by Celtic and Roman warriors before going into battle, which could account for its reputation as a courage enhancer, but actually it might be grounded in nutrition–borage is a great source of calcium and potassium GLA (gamma linolenic acid), an essential fatty acid contributing to brain, adrenal, and nervous system function.

If you love borage... you are intrepid and speak your mind. You're the kind of person who is not afraid to laugh out loud and find joy in the little things.

Oregano

The word oregano was derived from the Greek *oros ganos* meaning "joy of the mountains" and this fragrant, slightly spicy herb with pink and purple flowers is indeed a joyful sight. There are over 40 species of oregano and it grows wild in Europe and the Middle East on all sides of the Mediterranean, where it prefers chalky, crumbly soil.

Although it's said that Oregon got its name from the abundance of oregano growing wild there, that is not the case—it was more likely derived from Ouragon, the Native American name for what is now known as the Columbia River. The herb didn't become popular in North America until after World War II, when returning soldiers craved the flavor of the "pizza herb" they'd tasted overseas. It's now a key ingredient in sauces at pizza parlors everywhere.

Oregano is associated with Aphrodite the goddess of love, and ancient Greek women used the herb as a perfume to attract romance. The Romans followed suit and brides and grooms wore oregano wreaths to guarantee a happy future. It's said that if you put a sprig of oregano in your pillow you'll have psychic dreams and carrying some in your pocket will bring happiness.

Since the time of Hippocrates, oregano's oil has been used as a medicine to treat ailments, including dropsy (fluid retention) and poisoning. Modern herbalists recommend it as a treatment for winter flu, and recent scientific research is beginning to find evidence of its antiviral properties.

If you love oregano... people love to be around you! Your happiness is infectious and your ability to find and share the beauty in all things brings delight to everyone.

Eyebright

Its botanical name, *Euphrasia*, is for Euphrosyne or Euthymia—the goddess of joy and mirth, one of the three graces of ancient Greek mythology. Found in meadows through Europe and Asia, eyebright's white flowers are lightly veined with deep violet or black spots in the center, which resemble eyes. According to William Coles (1657) it was also called pigeon's grass because, "...Goldfinches, Linnets, and some other birds made use of this herb for the repairing of their loved ones' sight."

The connection between the form of the herb and its purpose persisted through the centuries in line with the theories of Swiss physician Paracelsus who asserted, "Nature marks each growth... according to its curative benefit." This idea was applied to eyebright by herbalist Reverend Hilderic Friend, who wrote in 1884: "...the purple and yellow spots and stripes which are upon the flowers of the Eyebright doth very much resemble the diseases of the eye, as bloodshot, etc., by which signature it hath been found out that this herb is effectual for the curing of the same."

Eyebright tea is still drunk as a folk remedy to improve vision and as an aid to enhance mental and psychic powers and memory. It's said one should carry a sprig of eyebright in their pocket when they need to find the truth in a situation.

If you love eyebright... you know that there's more than one way of seeing—with your eyes and with your heart. You're intuitive, joyful, and a seeker of truth.

"How canst thou gaze into these eyes of hers
Whom now thy heart delights in, and not see
Within each orb Love's philtred euphrasy
Make them of buried troth remembrancers?"

DANTE GABRIEL ROSSETTI, FROM *THE LOVE-MOON* (1869)

CHAPTER 3

—

Protection
& Guidance

Thyme

It's said that on Midsummer's Night the fairies dance in beds of wild thyme and the humans who place the flowers on their eyelids might be able to see the frolic. Traditionally a corsage of blue-violet thyme flowers signaled that the wearer was looking for a lover. The ancient Greeks used thyme in altar fires to sanctify offerings to the gods as well as to fumigate (the root of the Greek word *thymon* means "to fumigate") their spaces.

Drinking the tea or breathing thyme's perfume was thought to give one strength and courage. In medieval times, thyme was an emblem of bravery, and knights wore scarves embroidered with thyme leaves in tournaments. Courage may well be something needed in death, and the ancient Greeks put thyme in coffins to ensure safe passage into the underworld, believing that the dead inhabited thyme flowers as way stations along their journey. The ancient Egyptians incorporated it into the mummification process, and an English superstition says the spirits of the murdered rest in beds of thyme.

A tasty culinary herb, seasoning everything from pasta to potatoes, thyme is a favorite of bees, and its honey has a unique lovely flavor.

Thyme's volatile oil is called thymol and has been found to have powerful antioxidant and antimicrobial capabilities. Wild thyme makes a fine cough syrup, and an infusion with a pinch of salt is a hangover remedy.

If you love thyme... you see delight in all around you. You love a mystery and can keep a secret, and are never afraid of what the future holds.

"*I know a bank where the wild thyme blows.*"

WILLIAM SHAKESPEARE, FROM *A MIDSUMMER NIGHT'S DREAM*,
OBERON TO TITANIA

Loosestrife

FORGIVENESS | RECONCILIATION
WISHES GRANTED

Blooming Sally, milk willow-herb, rainbow weed, or willow sage—loosestrife has almost as many names as its cheery blossoms have colors. The plant's Latin name—*lysimachia*—is derived from the Greek words *lysis*, meaning "dissolution" and *mache*, meaning "strife."

This old-fashioned herb is not just beautiful, it's both a practical and magical ally in the garden and on the roadside. Grown around a home, loosestrife is said to enhance peace and drive away evil. There's a science to this that the medieval and ancient herbalists might not have realized. Loosestrife is a plant capable of phytoremediation, which means its roots absorb and remove pollutants, including metals and toxic chemicals, from soil. However, if you plant loosestrife, make sure to contain it, as it can be highly invasive.

It's said that the smoke of the dried herb drives away not just insects but, according to 16th-century herbalist Gerard "venomous beasts and serpents." It was also credited for curing cholera during outbreaks in England in the mid-19th century, saving hundreds of lives.

There's a superstition that suggests placing loosestrife flowers under yoked oxen makes them both submissive and gentle. What's good for beasts seems to benefit humans as well, since folklore also tells us that to resolve a disagreement we should give a gift of loosestrife to our adversary.

If you love loosestrife... you have a tender heart and help to put others at ease. You find the way to forgiveness no matter how perilous the path.

Verbena

ENCHANTMENT | PLEASANTRY | SENSITIVITY

Verbena's names are many and varied: vervain, *herba sacra*, the holy herb, Juno's tears, pigeon's grass, Christ's eye, wild clary, blue vervain, simpler's joy, and enchanter's plant.

Enchantment played a role in the Middle Ages when verbena was carried or worn for good luck. The Druids believed it to have magical properties and wove wreaths for women for protection. Ancient Roman priests used it to clean Jupiter's altars and expel evil from their homes. The Egyptians called it "Tears of Isis," and it's associated with the sacred in cultures from Persia to Scandinavia.

Also in the Middle Ages, verbena was tucked into pillows as an aphrodisiac. Young men and maidens wearing garlands of verbena with its white, pink, or blue flowers danced around bonfires on Christmas Eve. A gift of one of those garlands or wreaths was said to ensure fidelity, and later a present of a book with a verbena leaf pressed between the pages was a sign of courtship. These traditions may have inspired or been inspired by the proverb:

> ## "A verbena leaf sent to a lover
> ## Carries a message; you need no other."

Verbena is used as a treatment for stress, anxiety, and indigestion in both Chinese traditional and European herbal medicine. The herb's key compound, verbenalin, has been proven to have soporific properties. This may be why—because it makes you dreamy—verbena has been a symbol of enchantment used in divinations, rites, and incantations across cultures since ancient times.

If you love verbena... you're a peaceful soul with a tendency to daydream. Your powerful sense of wonder charms those who love you.

Cilantro

Cilantro and coriander are the same plant—the feathery leaf is cilantro and the seeds (which are really the fruit) are coriander (although, confusingly, the leaf is also called coriander in the UK). This herb was brought from the Mediterranean and Asia to the Americas by the conquistadores of Spain in the 1700s.

Its Asian roots may be the reason why cilantro also goes by the name "Chinese parsley" and legend says that eating this herb makes one immortal, while North African lore recommended cilantro leaves as a safeguard against the evil eye and to cure forgetfulness.

Magical or not, everyone has an opinion about the flavor of cilantro—some people adore it, while 4–14 percent of the world's population report that the leaf tastes like soap or worse. This is no accident—it's a genetic trait and research has linked hatred of cilantro to the genes that control scent receptor sites.

Fortunately, for curry lovers everywhere, this does not apply to the seed, which is its main ingredient. In fact, the flavor of coriander was compared to the bread of heaven (manna) in the Old Testament. The seeds are mentioned as an aphrodisiac in the Arabian Nights and used as an Iranian folk remedy for anxiety and insomnia.

Drinking a tea of crushed coriander seeds and dried cilantro leaves is said to ease anxiety and promote tranquility, and recent scientific studies have supported the sedative and muscle-relaxant capabilities of the chemical compounds within the herb.

If you love coriander... you never judge solely on appearances and have a talent for seeing both sides of a situation.

"And the house of Israel called the name thereof Manna: and it was like coriander seed, white; and the taste of it was like wafers made with honey."

Exodus 16:31

Skullcap

With blooms like the snapdragon, this purple-flowered perennial was most likely named for the shape of its blossoms. It is a member of the mint family and native to North America and parts of Europe. Skullcap favors sunny woodland patches. It's also called mad-dog weed because it was once believed to cure rabies.

Skullcap flowers look like something worn on the head, which is why it is also known as helmet flower, Quaker bonnet, and hood-wort. The herb's form reflects its target use as a treatment for disorders related to the head and mind. For centuries it has been used as an effective tranquilizer and soporific. Skullcap tea and tinctures have been deemed useful in the treatment of anxiety, insomnia, headaches, and even alcohol withdrawal.

The tea is said to stop nightmares and to guide those who consume it out of a dark night of the soul. Skullcap also has mild psychoactive properties, and was used as ceremonial plant smoked by Cherokee and other Native Americans to induce visions.

It is said that skullcap attracts love, and those who carry a sprig of it lead a life of grace, keeping their beloved faithful. The herb was used in magical spells to restore peace and calm.

If you love skullcap... you are thoughtful, although you have a tendency to live in your head. You have a gift for making connections between and with people.

"...they prick our fingers when we touch them; for they are not at all meant to be touched, but admired."

JOHN RUSKIN, FROM *PROSERPINA—STUDIES OF WAYSIDE FLOWERS* (1874)

Burdock

This cousin of the dandelion and thistle goes by many names: burr seed, cocklebur, fox's clote, beggar's buttons, cockle buttons, love leaves, and happy major. Shakespeare called it hardocks.

Because of its elegant form—heart-shaped leaves thicker at the base and sending off dramatic stalks—burdock has been a favorite of landscape painters beginning with the Dutch in the 17th century. Its burrs, or prickly spherical seedpods, stick to everything and George de Mestral, the Swiss inventor, is said to have gotten the inspiration for Velcro in the 1950s from burdock pods sticking to his dog's fur.

The second Friday in August is Burryman Day in Queensferry, near Edinburgh, Scotland. That's when a denizen of the town is completely covered in burdock burrs. Making his way with two attendants to pubs and city sites, this "Burry Man" parades without speaking like a slow-walking and prickly version of Frankenstein, as townspeople decorate him with flowers. It's said to be good luck to give the Burry Man money or whiskey.

Burdock lore recommends sprinkling the leaves around your home to guard against negativity. Or you can gather it in the waning moon and string bits of the root on red thread like beads as protection from evil.

In the 14th century, Hildegard of Bingen prescribed burdock as a cancer treatment. She was on to something as recent studies have shown a possibility that a chemical in burdock—*arctigenin*—may slow tumor growth and cell mutation.

If you love burdock... you know that beauty is more than skin deep and that a prickly exterior can guard a tender heart.

Milk Thistle

The spikey thistle flower of this herb is a bright pink, as pretty in bud as in bloom, but the plant was named milk thistle most probably for the veins of milky substance in the leaves. It's also known as ivory thistle and wild artichoke. Many of milk thistle's names—Mary-thistle, Saint Mary's thistle, and holy thistle—refer to the legend of how a few drops of milk fell from the Virgin Mary's breast, landed on a milk thistle leaf, and forever associated the herb with her.

It's said that boiling milk thistle and meditating while drinking the tea will attract good spirits, who can answer your most profound questions if you listen carefully. It's a protective herb and was believed to have the power to remove or break spells, repel snakes and thieves, and deflect lightning and negative energy.

Milk thistle's gift of protection applies to the medical, not just the magical. For over 2,000 years milk thistle has been used as a liver treatment and to purify the organs of toxins. Modern medicine supports this. It turns out that an active chemical that can be extracted from milk thistle seeds—silymarin—is a compound with the ability to repair cells in the liver that have been damaged by toxins, particularly alcohol. Beyond that, it can protect new liver cells from future destruction by these contaminants.

If you love milk thistle... you have a gentle spirit and a gift for healing. You do all that you can to prevent suffering in the world.

Horehound

RECOVERY | MENTAL POWERS | REASSURANCE

Native to Europe, North Africa, and Asia, horehound was introduced to North America by the early settlers. Although it may not be the fanciest herb in the garden, and this fuzzy crinkle-leaved perennial from the mint family may be perceived by some to be a weed, it is genuinely beautiful in its own way, and has been a favorite for millennia, not just because it repels destructive grasshoppers.

No herb is worth its muster if it doesn't offer some sort of magical protection, and horehound does not disappoint—since the Middle Ages it's been believed to safeguard those who carry it from witches' spells and charms.

It's a delightful flavoring for candy and a *digestif*. Horehound syrup has been used as an effective remedy for colds, coughs, and bronchitis for over 2,000 years and is still appreciated for its gentle healing ability. The ancient Roman physician Galen treated coughs and respiratory ailments with horehound. There's scientific evidence to support this, because the compound marrubiin in horehound has anti-microbial and anti-inflammatory properties.

Some say its name comes from the ancient Egyptians who popularized the herb and dedicated it to the primary god in their pantheon—Horus. Others say the name derives from the Old English *har hune*, evoking hoarfrost. In *Muses' Elyzium* (1630) early herbalist Michael Drayton had another explanation: "Here hore-hound 'gainst the mad dog's ill. By biting, never failing," because it was used to treat rabies.

If you love horehound... you are confident and steady, the kind of person others rely upon for both insight and guidance.

Rue

The word "rue" comes from the Greek for remembrance. Bunches of long-stemmed rue branches topped with tiny yellow flowers were dipped into holy water and shaken to bless the congregation during the celebration of Mass. That's likely why, in Shakespeare's *Hamlet*, Ophelia says: "There's rue for you, and here's some for me. We may call it 'herb of grace' o' Sundays."

Rue was said to improve the eyesight of painters and sculptors, and this belief persisted into the Renaissance—both Leonardo da Vinci and Michelangelo consumed rue to prevent eyestrain and foster inspiration. The *cimaruta* is a silver Italian folk charm shaped like rue, still worn as a pendant or hung in the home to ward off the evil eye. It's said that witches used rue to draw magic circles for casting spells. Yet, it was also the remedy for those spells, so bouquets were hung in homes to keep witches out.

In Marseilles during the plague, thieves used a vinegar infused with rue to protect themselves against any sickness that might be dwelling in the houses they robbed. According to *The Scientific American Cyclopedia of Formulas* (1910), the preparation combined fresh rue with dried rosemary tops, lavender flowers, camphor, garlic, cloves, and vinegar. "It is said that this medicated vinegar was invented by four thieves of Marseilles, who successfully employed it as a prophylactic during a visitation of pestilence."

If you love rue... you are slow to judge and quick to forgive. Your patience and gift for peacekeeping are treasured by the people around you, and you often bring calm to complicated situations.

*"Oh, the rue grows tall
and fair to see,
sweet 'herb of grace'
and memory."*

ARLO BATES, FROM *MEADOW RUE* (1892)

Solomon's Seal

Solomon's seal prefers shady forests to cultivated gardens and it's said that lily of the valley will only thrive in beds where Solomon's seal has been planted. If its roots are cut crosswise, the scars left behind resemble a six-pointed star, reminiscent of the seal of Solomon—the king described in both the Bible and the Quran, whose great wisdom matched his tremendous wealth. Legend had it that Solomon put his mark upon the plant when he recognized its importance for healing.

In magical lore, many herbs like Solomon's seal are grounding and grant protection—especially if you put the roots around your window frames—but this plant goes beyond that; it imbues users and those around them with supernatural powers. It is believed to help people weather change and make difficult decisions "with the wisdom of Solomon." In fact, a person anointed with the oil made from its roots is said to be as wise as King Solomon.

Although its shiny dark leaves and flowers shaped like stars or bells are poisonous, the roots of the herb have been used for centuries in both Western and Eastern medicine to make a tonic that is said to cure many ailments and fortify the body. A poultice of the leaves is used to soothe aches and pains and heal bruises.

If you love Solomon's seal... you're wise, of course, but also a thoughtful decision-maker, weighing all sides of the situation. You appreciate that wealth isn't always about money, and treasure the people and things in your life.

Mugwort

An herbaceous plant with feathery leaves and stalks of small white flowers, rich in pollen if not beauty, mugwort's name comes from the Old German *muggiwurti* meaning midge or fly root. The ancient Greeks used it to repel flies, moths, and other insects, and people still do. It is called springwort, because of a superstitious belief that it could magically open locks.

Also known as Saint John's Girdle, John the Baptist was said to have worn a belt of mugwort when he traveled into the wilderness. According to 16th-century herbalist Gerard, "Pliny saith that the traveller or wayfaring man that hath the herbe tied about him feeleth no wearisomnesse at all; and that he who hath it about him can be hurt by no poysonsome medicines, nor by any wilde beast, neither yet by the Sun itselfe..." This could be why travelers would put a leaf in a shoe or buttonhole for a happy journey, as well as the root of the saying: "If you put mugwort in your shoe you can run all day."

During the Middle Ages, it was thought that hanging a branch over your door would repel ghosts and the Devil, while putting it under the doorstep would drive away any undesirable mortals. If worn in a garland on Midsummer's Eve and then burned in a bonfire, the wearer's bad luck would burn with the herb. Those who gazed at that fire through a branch of mugwort would see a vision of the coming year.

If you love mugwort... you're a joyful soul always ready for an adventure. You respect the past, but are eager to see what the future may hold.

Ritual & Promise

Sage

S age's Latin name is *salvia officinalis*, meaning "safe and heal," with *officinalis* marking it as an official medicinal herb. A 1st-century saying has come down from the school of medicine that flourished in Salerno on the west coast of Italy (which interestingly welcomed students of all religions and genders): *Salvia salvatrix, natura conciliatrix*, or "sage the savior; nature the conciliator."

Superstition tells us that if you plant sage and keep it healthy, your finances will be vigorous as well. The smoke is used in many shamanic rituals. The incense produced from burning "smudge sticks" is believed to purify and sanctify the space. Lore tells us that sage is also a comfort to those in mourning. It was burnt at funerals or given as sachets for mourners to put under their pillow to help overcome grief.

Valued as a medicinal panacea since ancient times, sage confers longevity and perhaps immortality if one believes the proverb, "Why should a man die while sage grows in his garden?" Its volatile oil containing thujone and other enzymes, makes it an excellent anti-inflammatory and antiseptic. It has also been shown to enhance memory—most notably immediate recall—and there are ongoing studies to determine if sage can abate dementia. This possibility was first noted centuries ago by 16th-century John Gerard, who described sage as "singularly good for the head and brain. It quickeneth the senses and memory..."

If you love sage... you treasure gathering wisdom and sharing it with others. You're reliable and honest, and people find it easy to trust you.

Angelica

Growing across the Americas and from Korea to Lapland (where the stems are crafted into *fadnos*—reed flutes), angelica is one of the giants of the herb garden—reaching heights of 8 ft (2.5m). A useful herb in any medicine chest, angelica is a gentle treatment for a variety of ailments, especially coughs and bronchial disorders.

It is said to have gotten its name (formally *Archangelica officinalis*) when an angel appeared to a monk in a dream, telling him the herb was the cure for the Plague. The Germans used to call angelica "root of the Holy Ghost." Witches are said to hate this beautiful and aromatic herb with delicate white or pale green flowers that bloom on (or near) May 8—the feast day of St Michael, the archangel who appeared to the Virgin Mary. This inspired 16th-century poet Guillaume de Saluste Du Bartas to write:

"Contagious air, engendering pestilence,
Infect not those that in their mouths have ta'en
Angelica, that happy counter-bane
Sent down from heaven by some celestial scout…"

On the Faroe Islands, angelica stems are chopped into bits and served with cream and sugar, ostensibly for even more good luck. Garlands worn by children are said to protect them from danger. The juice of the plant is considered a remedy for all ailments. In Voodoo, angelica roots are used as a charm to bring blessings.

If you love angelica… you have a strong sense of purpose. You trust yourself and often find the best in a situation.

Dill

This herb, loved for its fragrant feathery foliage, is a favorite in the kitchen. It puts the zest in dill pickles (which have been a delicacy since at least the 17th century) because it's a natural food preservative. It's also a highlight in rice dishes, fish dishes, and sauces. In one form or another—delicate leaves, aromatic oil, or strong-flavored seed—dill is consumed or used for healing in most places in the world.

The word dill is derived from the Saxon *Dillan*, "to dull" for its soporific attributes or "lull" because it helped babies sleep, and dill water or weak tea is still given to treat colic. The ancient Roman physician Galen wrote that it "procureth sleep." Its reputation as a tranquilizer may be the source of the advice to hang bunches of dill over children's beds to protect them against nightmares and witches.

Bathing in dill and ginger tea is said to remove love hexes. During the Middle Ages, witches were said to concoct potions of dill, which when drunk would help end arguments and foster consent and friendship.

Eating dill or drinking a tea made from the seeds continues to be recommended as a treatment for insomnia. When it comes to healing uses, it's primarily the seed herbalists focus on. Because of its mildness, it is a popular favorite in traditional Chinese medicine, and is used by Ayurvedic healers for stomach aches.

If you love dill... you are a calming influence upon the people around you but don't lack for sparkle and spontaneity—always game for an adventure.

Trefoil, vervain, John's wort, dill,
Hinder witches of their will.

SAYING

Bay Laurel

ASSURED HAPPINESS | GLORY | THE REWARD OF MERIT

This herb, *Laurus nobilis*, with attributes medicinal, culinary, and even magical, can be found in bottles at your local grocery store labeled as bay leaves. A pot of this sturdy evergreen shrub with tiny white flowers is said to ward off evil and assure happiness if left on your doorstep. Bay laurel keeps moths out of closets, weevils out of flour, and is said to come in handy during exorcisms. In his *Complete Herbal*, the 17th-century writer Nicholas Culpeper credited it with yet another power:

"... neither witch nor devil, thunder nor lightning, will hurt a man in the place where a bay-tree is."

In Greek mythology, it's the herb of the goddess Daphne—the nymph who transformed herself into a bay laurel tree to avoid the amorous pursuit of the god Apollo—and, as such, is connected with purity. The Oracle of Delphi is said to have eaten crushed bay leaves to make her visions more powerful. In ancient Greece, it was woven into wreaths for athletes, heroes, scholars (leading to baccalaureate), and poets (giving us poet laureate).

Ancient Greek doctors carried laurel with them while treating patients because its energy or presence in a sickroom was believed to help heal so many ailments. It was also burned as an incense or fumigant to purify the air. To this day the oil is rubbed into muscles and joints to ease aches and stiffness.

If you love bay laurel... you strive to do your best and usually end up excelling. Although you're practical and reliable, you also have the gift of seeing the magic in everyday things.

Parsley

Parsley is frustratingly slow to germinate. There's an old saying, "Parsley goes down to Hades nine times before it comes up." Perhaps because of this, Greeks associated it with Persephone, the goddess who personifies vegetation, and guided souls to the underworld. This may be why it's still served at funeral meals.

A sprig of parsley is commonly used as a garnish on a dinner plate, and with good reason—the Romans believed it would guard food from poisoning and contamination. Although this may be apocryphal, it served a dual purpose, and as early as CE 164, the Greek physician Galen recorded that parsley was a digestive herb, both "sweet and grateful to the stomach." It's a breath freshener as well, for as Thomas Hill noted in 1511, "There is nothing that doth like sweeten the mouth, as fresh and green Parcely eaten." Parsley is packed with vitamins, having three times the amount of vitamin C per serving as oranges.

Dreaming of eating parsley is believed to be a good omen. It was said to make witches' brooms fly. Lore has it that the pixies once had a beautiful tulip bower in West Devon where the flowers had a fragrance lovelier than a rose, but when it was replaced with parsley they tore the leaves ragged, and continue to do so—explaining the plant's scruffy edges.

If you love parsley... you are patient and wise. You're equally happy at large parties or spending time alone and are always up for taking on a new project or adventure.

Turmeric

A member of the ginger family, turmeric is native to India and Asia, but is growing increasingly popular in the West. It's known as "golden spice" or the "spice of life," not because of its remarkable red-orange flowers resembling lilies, but for the yellow of its rhizome, or roots, for which it is cultivated. In Indian Ayurvedic medicine, turmeric is called curcumin—connected to the Sanskrit word for yellow. It's a natural dye used to color everything from Buddhist monks' robes to commercially manufactured mustard.

Turmeric has cultural and religious significance throughout Southeast Asia. Indian folklore tells of the fragrance of turmeric driving away ghosts. Brides and grooms are painted with *haldi* paste—a fragrant mixture of turmeric and sandalwood powder—during wedding festivities to invite fertility and prosperity. It's sprinkled inside traditional Hindu homes to bless and purify them, but it is also said that accidentally spilling turmeric on the ground can attract misfortune.

Turmeric has been the subject of a great deal of scientific research—over 1,500 accredited studies—that suggests that it has tremendous potential as an anti-inflammatory, a treatment for cancer, arthritis, and heart disease, and a supplement that lowers cholesterol and enhances immunity. This makes curry—in which turmeric is a primary spice—a potent healing food.

If you love turmeric... you have a warm heart and a sunny disposition. You bring healing and happiness and a sense of abundance to everyone you love.

Kava

Kava is propagated by dividing the roots, because the tiny male flowers are sterile and the female flowers extremely rare. This shrub with heart-shaped leaves has been used in rituals in Polynesia, Hawaii, and other islands of the South Pacific for centuries. It's imbibed in a ceremonial tea made by grounding the roots to a pulp and steeping them in cold water. Kava is shared as a gesture of hospitality and friendship in "kava circles" and thought to bring good luck and ward off evil, as well as inducing a blissful state.

The 18th-century explorer Captain James Cook was probably the first to bring it to the attention of British herbalists. The preparation of the drink was described by a naturalist who traveled with him—George Forster: "This root is cut small, and the pieces chewed by several people, who spit the macerated mass into a bowl, where some water of coconuts is poured upon it. They then strain it through a quantity of fibers of coconuts, squeezing the chips, till all their juices mix with the coconut-milk; and the whole liquor is decanted into another bowl."

Kava became popular in the United States in the 1990s as a stress reliever. The primary active ingredients in the root are kavalactones, which work like a low dose of Valium, but are not addictive. Recent studies have reported success in using kava as a muscle relaxant and to treat anxiety, insomnia, and even convulsions.

If you love kava... you're personable and engaged, as happy telling stories as listening to them. You're a protector and guide to the people around you, always willing to help them find their way out of challenging situations.

"Thou pretty herb of Venus' tree
Thy true name is yarrow
Now who my bosom friend must be,
Pray tell thou me tomorrow."

FOLK RHYME

Yarrow

**EFFECTIVENESS I BRAVERY
CURE FOR THE HEARTACHE**

White and lilac, yellow and deep burgundy, what some see as a roadside weed speaks to others of a noble history in wars and prophecy. Yarrow patches grow stronger and thicker every year, which is why the herb symbolized longevity for the ancient Chinese. The association with long life may be why it was planted around Confucius's grave. Yarrow stalks harvested there are said to have the best energy for divination by those who practice the *I Ching*, or *Book of Changes*. The sticks are sorted and tossed in a specific manner and the hexagrams they form of six yin (broken) or yang (unbroken) lines are read to tell the future and answer a seeker's questions.

Yarrow's mystical side spans the globe. European wisdom recommends harvesting it on Midsummer's Day for magical uses. It was also sewn into little pillows to induce dreams of one's future love.

Many of yarrow's names allude to its lore: sanguinary, soldier's woundwort, herb militaris, and staunchweed. It's said that Achilles learned of the wound-healing powers of yarrow from the mythical Chiron the centaur, and taught the Ancient Greeks to use yarrow poultices to staunch wounds in battles of the Trojan War. Called *achillée* in French, it's grown near toolsheds and carpenters' shops as a first-aid treatment for scrapes and cuts. The Ute Indian warriors made the same discovery, naming yarrow "wound medicine."

If you love yarrow... you have an inner strength and outward bravery that sometimes obscures your tender heart. You're resilient with a gift for balancing your life, especially the practical with the sacred.

Mullein

Mullein is called flannel flower, feltwort, hare's beard, and beggar's blanket (for its velvety leaves, which were wrapped around the neck to avert a sore throat). It's also known as torch flower and candlewick plant from stories of Roman soldiers dipping the yellow-flowered stalks into animal tallow to make torches for their camps, a practice that continued throughout Europe when the stems were repurposed as candlewicks. Superstitions tell of witches lighting stalks during their Sabbaths, yet mullein was also a charm against demons.

The seeds are toxic and narcotic, but were used by early Native Americans when fishing. They tossed them into rivers and lakes for fish to eat—the fish would become dazed and easier to catch. There's an Irish superstition that if you put mullein in the churn after butter has turned, you can reconstitute the butter. Herbalists across cultures now recommend mullein as a respiratory remedy, useful for colds, coughs, and bronchitis.

This Old-World plant now grows in abundance in the United States. Its yellow flowers have been used as dye since Roman times—both for fabrics and lightening hair—the ancient equivalent of the bottle blonde. As the English herbalist John Parkinson wrote in 1629: mullein flowers "boyled in lye dyeth the haires of the head yellow and maketh them faire and smooth." Mixing in sulfuric acid to reduce the pH content turns the dye green, a different sort of style choice.

If you love mullein... you are soft-hearted and quietly confident. Your inner strength supports and guides the people closest to you.

Tansy

Tansy's name comes from a corruption of the Greek for immortality or deathless—*athanatos* means undying. This may be because the clusters of golden button-shaped flowers are especially long-lasting. Or it's because tansy was used to line coffins and preserve the bodies within them. Magical lore tells of the leaves being tucked around bodies before funerals to ensure the soul a peaceful journey to the afterworld.

A drink brewed from tansy was said to make the Greek god Zeus's cupbearer Ganymede immortal, and people drink tansy wine to this day as a pleasant beverage that eases a sore throat and may even treat diabetes. Whether tansy indeed assures eternal life or not, it does encourage growth of the plants around it in the garden, and is beneficial to sow near beans, cucumbers, corn, potatoes, raspberries, roses, and squash, because the herb helps to concentrate potassium in the soil.

Tansy puddings are eaten after fasting during Lent. According to 19th-century herbalist, Mrs M. Grieve: "These Tansy cakes were made from the young leaves of the plant, mixed with eggs, and were thought to purify the humours of the body after the limited fare of Lent."

Also called "bitter buttons," perhaps because the flowers smell a lot like camphor, tansy is said to bind people for life. However, be cautious: giving a gift of tansy in some parts of Italy may be perceived as an insult.

If you love tansy... you are lively and helpful and possess a gift for anticipating the impact your ideas and actions could have on the future.

Mint

The pleasure of an after-dinner mint began when the first forager plucked a leaf and enjoyed the menthol bite as well as the ease it brought to digestion. Mint is a primary herb that grows all over the world. There are over 25 species and 600 varieties of mint, including the perennial favorites peppermint and spearmint, although medicinally, peppermint tends to be more potent.

In the Middle East, particularly Morocco, mint tea—made with fresh mint, dried green tea, and lots of sugar—is prepared in a ceremonial manner, and is always offered to welcome guests. Refusing it is thought to be impolite. Tea bars are gathering places in the Middle East, much as cafes and pubs are in other parts of the world.

It's used to flavor many products, such as chewing gum and toothpaste, and the tea and volatile oil are reliable treatments for upset stomachs and related ailments. Mint calms the digestive muscles, as well as diminishing colds and headaches. In laboratory studies, it's been proven to kill some types of bacteria and viruses, suggesting that more research is merited.

Greek mythology tells of Persephone, who changed her rival Menthe into a plant, jealous of the attention her husband Pluto (the god of the underworld) was lavishing on the nymph. Menthe became mint—not the most beautiful herb in the garden, but one which, when stepped on, releases a delightful fragrance. Ironically, there are those who also say mint is an aphrodisiac.

If you love mint... you're loyal and convivial although occasionally opinionated. You have a welcoming home and a gift for hospitality.

"When the yellow broom is ripe
Upon its native soil,
It's like a pretty baby bright
With sweet and wavily smile."

FOLK SONG

Broom

ARDOR I MIRTH I SPELLS

Broom is a yellow-flowered herb with stiff stems, which indeed looks like the sweeping implement for which it is named. Many believe that form followed function because binding the tufted stalks made the plant an effective tool for sweeping. Others say its appellation was derived from its association with witches, who used the herb in flying spells. It is thought that because an overdose of the active element in broom—sparteine—can cause dangerous heart arrhythmia and excess excitability, this may have led to the stories about witches wildly cackling and swooping about on their brooms. However, because of the effects of sparteine, recent studies have shown that extract of broom has promise in treating low blood pressure and related heart disease.

There are several superstitions associated with the herb. Sweeping with it at the wrong time of year could be bad luck, as cautioned in the rhyme: "If you sweep the house with blossomed broom in May, you are sure to sweep the head of the house away." It was also thought to calm an anxious person and put them to sleep if waved over them, leading to another adage: "Strew it at his head and feet, and the thicker that ye do strew, the sounder he will sleep." Others say that smoking broom can lead to hallucinations.

Besides these magical abilities, broom also has a practical application: grown on sandy banks and slopes, its tight root structure prevents erosion.

If you love broom... you're a bit of a homebody, but in the best sort of way—creating a place that's not only lovely but conducive to creativity and friendship.

Hemp

FATE I MEDITATION I INSIGHT

Hemp, also known as *cannabis sativa*—recently legalized in much of the United States—is enjoying a renewed popularity as a healing herb, but it's been appreciated for millennia, and not only by those seeking a mystical or mind-altering experience. Believed to have originated north of the Himalayas, it was long cultivated in the fenlands of Great Britain, and brought to the Americas by European explorers.

Herodotus wrote of the Scythians using it in funerary rites—covering hot stones with the seeds and inhaling the smoke for purification-producing hallucinations, and it appears in Chinese pharmaceutical texts by the Chinese Emperor Shen Nung dating back as far as 2737 BCE.

The medicinal element is concentrated in the resin from the buds of the seedy cream-colored flowers. When smoked, the drug is known by many names throughout the world: hashish, beng, kif, dagga, ganga, and marijuana. It is an effective analgesic, and non-psychoactive cannabidiol (hemp oil) is growing in popularity as a treatment for everything from arthritis to cancer, and even epilepsy.

Hemp has other uses—the fiber for rope and fabric, and the seeds for bird food and soap. It is said that hemp plants grown from seeds sown on Midsummer's Eve or Halloween can be used to attract love, especially when reciting:

*"Hempseed I set, hempseed I sow
The man that is my true love
Come after me and mow."*

If you love hemp... you're a dreamer. You come up with wonderful ideas and creative solutions to challenges and are happy to share your insights with those around you.

Tarragon

Its Latin name—*Artemisia dracunculus*—alludes to the Greek moon goddess Artemis (Diana to the Romans), who was said to have presented tarragon to the centaur Chiron. Pliny the Elder, in his *Natural History*, ascribes the beginnings of the study of botany and pharmacology to this oracle and son of Cronus (Saturn) and Philyra. The second half of the name—*dracunculus* or "little dragon"—signifies its promise to cure the bites of venomous beasts both actual and mythical.

Called "the king of herbs," it's a favorite in French cookery, with an elegant and distinctive flavor. Legend says that St Catherine first brought tarragon to France in the 14th century, but it is not exclusive to that country—varieties can be found in Europe, Asia, and India, as well as the American southwest and Mexico.

Writing in 1884, Richard Folkard quoted the herbalist Gerard, "The ancient herbalists affirmed that the seed of Flax put into a Radish root, or Sea Onion and so set would bring forth the herb Tarragon." They got part of it right—it's almost impossible to grow French tarragon from seeds, but Sea Onions aren't required—only a division of roots in the spring.

Tarragon has been used since ancient times to treat a toothache. Native Americans used the wild variety to treat colds and dysentery. Rich in vitamins and other nutrients, it is a healthful dietary supplement. It's also an antioxidant, and tarragon added to tea or vinegar can be useful in relieving anxiety and stress.

If you love tarragon... you are just as fond of travel as you are of returning home. You have refined taste for all things food and cultural and just enough stubbornness to stand up for yourself.

BIBLIOGRAPHY

Ambrose, Dawn C P, Annamalai Manickavasagan, Ravindra Naik, eds. *Leafy Medicinal Herbs: Botany, Chemistry, Postharvest Technology and Uses*. Oxfordshire: CABI, 2016. Kindle e-book.

Aneira, Crystal. *Herbal Riot*. (website) Accessed September 6, 2017. http://herbalriot.tumblr.com

Arrowsmith, Nancy. *Essential Herbal Wisdom: A Complete Exploration of 50 Remarkable Herbs*. Woodbury, Minnesota: Llewellyn Publications, 2009.

Beals, Katherine. *Flower Lore and Legend*. New York: H. Holt, 1917. https://hdl.handle.net/2027/wu.89031213754

Betti, Georges and Mathias Schmidt. "Devil's Claw: Myths and Facts About Its Discovery" *The International Society for Phyto-Sciences* (website) Accessed September 6, 2017. http://phytosciences.org/en/news/209-devil-s-claw-myths-and-facts-about-its-discovery

Chevalier, Andrew. *The Encyclopedia of Medicinal Plants*. London: Dorling Kindersley, 1996.

Choukas-Bradley, Melanie and Tina Thieme Brown. *An Illustrated Guide to Eastern Woodland Wildflowers and Trees: 350 Plants Observed at Sugarloaf Mountain, Maryland*. Charlottesville: University of Virginia Press, 2004.

Cortambert, Louise. *The Language of Flowers*. Philadelphia: Lea & Blanchard, 1839. https://hdl.handle.net/2027/nyp.33433010841298

Cunningham, Scott. *Encyclopedia of Magical Herbs*. Woodbury, Minnesota: Llewellyn Publications, 1985.

Dana, Mrs. William Starr. *How to Know the Wild Flowers*. Boston: Phillips, Sampson, and Company. https://hdl.handle.net/2027/njp.32101068974755

Dumont, Henrietta. *The Floral Offering: A Token of Affection and Esteem; Comprising the Language and Poetry of Flowers*. Philadelphia: H. C. Peck & T. Bliss, 1852. https://hdl.handle.net/2027/coo1.ark:/13960/t5bc4jc61

Earle, Alice Mores. *Old-Time Gardens*. New York: The Macmillan Company, 1902. http://www.gutenberg.org/files/39049/39049.txt

Eastman, John, and Amelia Hansen. *The Book of Forest & Thicket: Trees, Shrubs, and Wildflowers of Eastern North America*. Mechanicsburg, Pennsylvania: Stackpole Books, 1992.

Eat the Invaders (website) Accessed September 6, 2017. http://eattheinvaders.org

Esling, Lady Catharine Harbeson Waterman. *Flora's Lexicon: An Interpretation of the Language and Sentiment of Flowers*. 1839. https://hdl.handle.net/2027/hvd.32044021117809

Farlex. *The Free Dictionary: Medical Dictonary*. (website) http://medical-dictionary.thefreedictionary.com

Field, Ann. *The Meaning of Herbs: Myth, Language & Lore*. San Francisco: Chronicle Books LLC, 2015. Kindle edition.

Folkard, Richard. *Plant Lore, Legends, and Lyrics*. London: Sampson, Lowe, Marston, Searle, and Rivington, 1884. PDF e-book.

Foster, Steven and James A. Duke. *Peterson's Field guide to Medicinal Plants and Herbs of Eastern and Central North America*. Boston: Houghton Mifflin Harcourt, 2014.

Friend, Hilderic. *Flowers and Flower Lore*. Vol. I. London: W. Swan Sonnenschein and Co., 1884.

Gibbons, Euell. *Stalking the Healthful Herbs*. New York: McKay, 1966.

Gordon, Sue. *Plant Names Explained: Botanical Terms and Their Meaning*. Cincinnati: David & Charles, 2007.

Gray, Samantha. *The Secret Language of Flowers*. London: CICO Books, 2015.

Greenway, Kate. *Language of Flowers*. New York: Dover Publications, 1992. Originally published Avenel, 1884.

Grieve F.R.H.S., Mrs. Maud Grieve. *The Medicinal, Culinary, Cosmetic and Economic Properties, Cultivation and Folk-Lore of Herbs, Grasses, Fungi, Shrubs & Trees with their Modern Scientific Uses*. New York: Dover Publications, 1971. Originally published Harcourt Brace, 1931. http://www.botanical.com/botanical/mgmh/mgmh.html

Hardy Herbs (website) Accessed September 6, 2017. https://hardyherbs.com/

Harper; Douglas, ed. *Online Entymology Dictionary*. Etymonline (website) www.etymonline.com

Heptinstall, S. and D. V. C. Awang. "Feverfew: A Review of Its History, Its Biological and Medicinal Properties, and the Status of Commercial Preparations of the Herb." *Phytomedicines of Europe*. April 15, 1998, 158-175. DOI:10.1021/bk-1998-0691.ch013

Herb Wisdom (website) Accessed September 6, 2017. www.herbwisdom.com

Hill M.D., John. *Useful Family Herbal and History of Plants*. London: W. Owen. 1770. https://archive.org/details/mobot31753002739453

Hoffman, Frank and Martin J. Manning. *Herbal Medicine and Botanical Medical Fads*. Routledge: 2014. Kindle e-book.

Hopkins, Albert A. *The Scientific American Cyclopedia of Formulas*. New York: Munn & Co., 1919.

Johannsen, Kristin. *Ginseng Dreams: The Secret World of America's Most Valuable Plant*. The University Press of Kentucky, 2006. Kindle e-book.

Kaldera, Raven. *Northern Tradition Shamanism* (website) Accessed September 6, 2017. http://www.northernshamanism.org

Kleager, Brenda Jenkins. *Secret Meaning of Flowers*. Treasured Secrets Publishing Company. Huntsville, Alabama, 2013.

Koulivand, Peir Hossein, Maryam Khaleghi Ghadiri, and Ali Gorji. "Lavender and the Nervous System." *Evidence-based Complementary and Alternative Medicine: eCAM* 2013 (2013): 681304. PMC. (Website) Accessed September 6, 2017.

Kowalchik, Claire, William H Hylton; Anna Carr; et al eds. *Rodale's Illustrated Encyclopedia of Herbs*. Emmaus, Pennsylvania: Rodale Press, 1998.

Kress, Henriette. *Henrietta's Herbal* (website) Accessed September 6, 2017. http://www.henriettes-herb.com

Language and Poetry of Flowers. London: Milner and Sowerby, 1867. https://hdl.handle.net/2027/uc1.31175035216707

Lebot, Vincent, Mark Merlin, and Lamont Lindstrom *Kava: The Pacific Elixir: The Definitive Guide to Its Ethnobotany, History, and Chemistry*. Simon and Schuster, 1997. Kindle e-book.

Lehner, Ernest and Johanna Lehner. *Folklore and Symbolism of Flowers, Plants, and Trees*. New York: Dover Publications, 2003.

Loy, Susan. *Flowers, the Angels' Alphabet: The Language and Poetry of Flowers*. Golden Colorado: CSL Press, 2001.

Lust, John. *The Herb Book*. New York: Dover Publications, 2014.

Mabey, Richard. *Weeds: In Defense of Nature's Most Unloved Plants*. New York: Ecco, 2012.

Mossendew, Jane. *Thorn, Fire and Lily: Gardening with God in Lent and Easter*. A&C Black: 2004.

Mother Earth Living. *Plant Profile*. (website) Accessed September 6, 2017. http://www.motherearthliving.com/plant-profile

Mountain Rose Herbs (website) Accessed September 6, 2017. https://www.mountainroseherbs.com

Nature Gate. "Plants" (website) Accessed September 6, 2017. http://www.luontoportti.com/suomi/en/kasvit/

Northcote, Lady Rosalind. *The Book of Herbs.* London, New York: J. Lane, 1903. https://archive.org/details/cu31924073899373

Oldmeadow, Katherine L. *The Folklore of Herbs.* Birmingham: Cornish Brothers Limited, 1946.

Our Herb Garden. "History and Folklore." (website) Accessed September 6, 2017. http://www.ourherbgarden.com/herb-history.html

Pappas, Stephanie. "25 Odd Facts about Marijuana." *Live Science* (website), November 22, 2016. https://www.livescience.com/56600-odd-facts-marijuana.html

Rigsby, Gem. *Herb Seed for Thought.* Texas: Spur Ridge Press, 1998.

Rohde, Eleanour Sinclair. *The Old English Herbals.* London: Longmans, Green and Co., 1922. https://hdl.handle.net/2027/uiug.30112104110132

Royal Botanic Gardens, Kew (website) Accessed September 6, 2017. https://www.kew.org

Saul, Florence. *Herb Dictionary* (website) Accessed September 6, 2017. http://www.auntyflo.com/herb-dictionary

Seaton, Beverly. *The Language of Flowers: A History.* University of Virginia Press, 1995.

Shakespeare, William. *The Arden Shakespeare.* Edited by Kenneth Muir. London: Methuen, 1962. shakespeare.mit.edu

Silverthorne, Elizabeth. *Legends and Lore of Texas Wildflowers.* (Louise Lindsey Merrick Natural Environment Series) Texas: A&M University Press, 2003. Kindle e-book.

Smart, Christopher. "Jubilate Agno." (website) Accessed September 6, 2017. http://www.pseudopodium.org/repress/jubilate/agno-c-frames.html

Staub, Jack. *75 Exceptional Herbs for Your Garden.* Gibbs Smith, 2008. Kindle edition.

The New England Farmer and Horticultural Register. Boston: J. Nourse, 1860. https://hdl.handle.net/2027/uc1.31175012071158

Thomas, Joseph. *A Comprehensive Medical Dictionary.* Philadelphia: J.B. Lippincott & Company, 1886. https://hdl.handle.net/2027/uc1.b4210497

Thoreau, Henry David. *Walden.* New York: Thomas Y. Crowell & Company, 1910. PDF e-book.

University of Maryland Medical Center. "Complementary and Alternative Medicine Guide." (website) Accessed September 6, 2017. http://www.umm.edu/health/medical/altmed

Vickery, Roy. *Plant-Lore: Collecting the Folklore and Uses of Plants.* (website) Accessed September 6, 2017. http://www.plant-lore.com

Wait, Minnie Curtis. *Among Flowers and Trees with the Poets: Or, The Plant Kingdom In Verse; A Practical Cyclopaedia for Lovers of Flowers.* Boston: Lee, 1901. https://hdl.handle.net/2027/hvd.hw2bxl

Watts, D.C. *Dictionary of Plant Lore.* Academic Press, 2007. Kindle edition.

Witchipedia. "Alphabetical List of Magickal and Healing Herbs" (website) Accessed September 6, 2017. http://www.witchipedia.com/main:herbs

Wood, Matthew. *The Earthwise Herbal, Volume II: A Complete Guide to New World Medicinal Plants.* Berkeley, California: North Atlantic Books, 2009.

ACKNOWLEDGMENTS

Many thanks to Cindy Richards, Kristine Pidkameny, Carmel Edmonds, and all the lovely people at CICO Books. Huge gratitude as well to Sarah Perkins for her illustrations, and Maggie Beiting and Joel Parrish for always being up for a trip to the lavender farm.